These Are My Senses

T0101114

What Can I Feel?

Joanna Issa

Heinemann
LIBRARY
Chicago, Illinois

© 2015 Heinemann Library
an imprint of Capstone Global Library, LLC
Chicago, Illinois

All rights reserved. No part of this publication may be reproduced or transmitted in any form or by any means, electronic or mechanical, including photocopying, recording, taping, or any information storage and retrieval system, without permission in writing from the publisher.

Edited by Siân Smith
Designed by Richard Parker and Peggie Carley
Picture research by Tracy Cummins
Production by Victoria Fitzgerald
Originated by Capstone Global Library Ltd

Library of Congress Cataloging-in-Publication Data
Cataloging-in-publication information is on file with the Library of Congress.
ISBN 978-1-4846-0432-8 (paperback)
ISBN 978-1-4846-0445-8 (eBook PDF)

Image Credits
Getty Images: JuanSilva, 17, LWA/Dann Tardif, cover, moxiegirl12, 11, back cover, Salima Senyavskaya, 14, will_snyder, 7; Shutterstock: auremar, 19, Dhoxax, 12, Diana Taliun, 16, 20 (left), George Lamson, 4, Igor Kovalchuk, 15, 21 (left), ipag, 6, JCREATION, 8, Monika Gniot, 13, oksix, 18, 21 (right), Sunny Forest, 10, vidguten, 5, 22 (left), Whitear, 9, 20 (right), 22 (right)

Every effort has been made to contact copyright holders of material reproduced in this book. Any omissions will be rectified in subsequent printings if notice is given to the publisher.

Printed in the United States 6035

Contents

What Can I Feel? 4
Quiz: Opposite Pairs 20
Picture Glossary. 22
Index 22
Notes For Teachers
and Parents 23
In This Book 24

What Can I Feel?

Here is a puppy.

It feels **soft**.

Here is some gum.

It feels sticky.

Here is a cactus.

It feels **spiky**.

Here is a tree.

It feels rough.

Here is a flower.

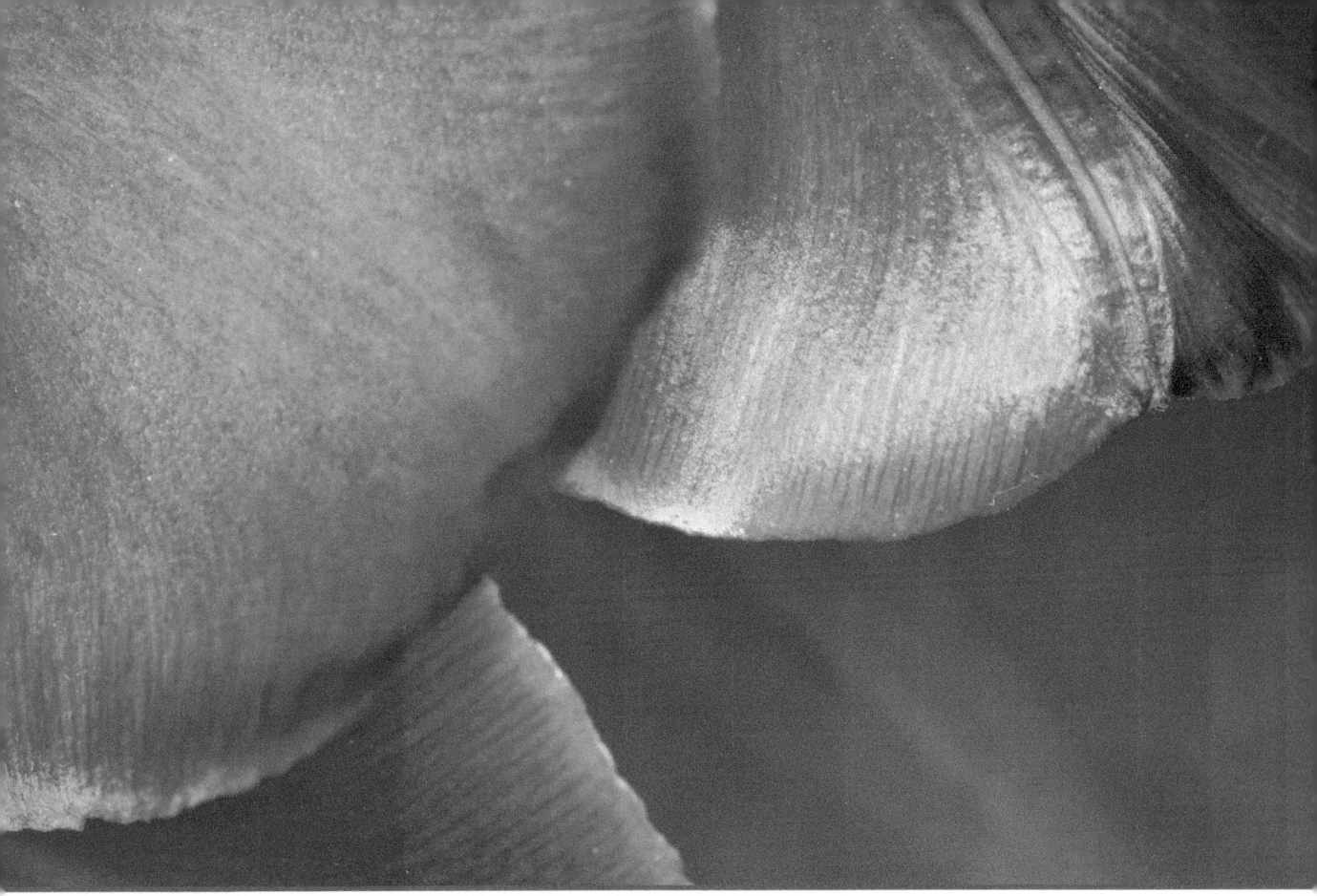

It feels smooth.

Here is a leaf.

It feels rough.

Here is play dough.

It feels soft.

Here is honey.

It feels sticky.

Quiz: Opposite Pairs

Which of these objects feels spiky?

Which of these objects feels sticky?

21 The cactus feels spiky.
The honey feels sticky.

Picture Glossary

soft

spiky

Index

cactus 8

flower 12

gum 6

honey 18

leaf 14

play dough 16

puppy 4

tree 10

Notes For Teachers and Parents

BEFORE READING

Build Background:

Have children think of things that are soft to touch and things that are rough. Which do they like to feel best?

AFTER READING

Recall and reflection:

What things are soft to touch? (puppy, play dough) What things are sticky? (honey, gum) Would children like to touch something sticky? Why or why not?

Sentence knowledge:

Ask children to look at page 12. How many sentences are on this page? How can they tell?

Word knowledge (phonics):

Encourage children to point at the word *feels* on page 13. Sound out the four phonemes in the word *f/ee/l/s.* Ask children to sound out each phoneme as they point at the letters and then blend the sounds together to make the word *feels.* Challenge them to say some words that rhyme with *feels.* (heels, meals, peels, wheels)

Word recognition:

Have children point to the word *rough* on page 11. Can they also find it on page 15?

EXTENDING IDEAS

Put a number of small objects in a bag. (toy car, block, soft toy, pencil, eraser, sock) Ask children to put their hands inside the bag and feel for an object. Can they describe how it feels to the other children? Can the other children guess what the object is? Let children pull the object out of the bag to show the class if they were right or wrong.

In This Book

Topic

touch and senses

High-frequency words

a

here

is

it

Sentence stems

1. It feels _____.
2. Here is a _____.